D1071045

From a Tiny Seed to a Mighty Tree

How Plants Grow

by Ruth Owen

Ruby Tuesday Books

Published in 2017 by Ruby Tuesday Books Ltd.

Editor: Mark J. Sachner
Designer: Emma Randall
Consultant: Judy Wearing, PhD, BEd
Production: John Lingham

Photo credits:
Alamy: 9 (bottom left), 22 (top); FLPA: 22 (bottom), 23 (bottom); Istock Photo: 29 (center); Shutterstock: Cover, 1, 2–3, 4–5, 6–7, 8–9, 10–11, 12–13, 14–15, 16–17, 18–19, 20–21, 23 (top), 24–25, 26–27, 30–31.

Library of Congress Control Number: 2016918439

ISBN 978-1-911341-29-1

Printed and published in the United States of America

For further information including rights and permissions requests, please contact our Customer Service Department at 877-337-8577.

Contents

Words shown in **bold** in the text are explained in the glossary.

The download button shows there are free worksheets or other resources available. Go to:

www.rubytuesdaybooks.com/getstarted

Autumn Acorns

It's autumn in a park.

Squirrel

A squirrel is eating acorns that drop from oak trees.

Acorn

The squirrel buries some of the acorns in the ground.

When winter comes, there is not much food around.

The squirrel digs up some of her buried acorns and eats them.

She doesn't find all the acorns, though...

Let's Talk

What do you think might happen to the acorns that stay buried in the ground?

A New Oak Tree

The buried acorns wait for winter to end.

In spring, the sunshine warms up the soil.

Under the ground, a tiny **shoot** sprouts from an acorn.

Shoot

Acorn

Inside an acorn there is an oak tree seed. The seed contains all the material needed to grow a new tree.

Oak tree
seedling

Leaf

The shoot pushes up
through the soil and
into the sunshine.

After a few weeks, the
shoot has grown into an
oak tree **seedling** with
roots, a stem, and leaves.

Stem

The seedling takes in
water from the soil
through its roots.

Roots

Growing and Changing

The years go by, and the little oak tree seedling grows.

Its stem becomes a thick trunk with long branches.

Branch

Trunk

When it is about 50 years old, the tree begins to grow acorns.

An Oak Tree's Life Cycle

A 100-year-old oak tree

An oak tree may live for hundreds of years.

An acorn drops from the tree and grows in the soil.

The story of how a living thing grows and changes is called its life cycle.

A 50-year-old oak tree

After one year, the seedling is 20 inches (0.5 m) tall.

A seedling grows from the acorn.

Growing Sunflowers

A tree may take many years to grow from a seed. Other plants, such as sunflowers, grow in just a few months.

Sunflower

Sunflower seeds

Seeds contain a store of food. Seedlings use this food to help them grow.

A Sunflower's Life Cycle

A person plants a seed in soil in spring.

After four weeks, a seedling grows.

In late summer, seeds form in the center of the flower—ready to make new plants next spring.

Let's Draw It!

Draw the life cycle of a sunflower.

Use the pictures on this page to help you.

Add these labels to your drawing.

Seed   **Seedling**   **Leaf**
Bud   **Flower**

The seedling gets taller and grows leaves.

The bud becomes a flower.

In early summer, a flower bud forms.

Animal Helpers

Flowers produce a dust called **pollen** that is needed for making seeds.

Many plants need pollen from another plant of the same kind before they can produce seeds.

How does pollen get from one flower to another?

Lily flower

Petal

Pollen dust

When a bee visits a flower, pollen sticks to its body.

Then the bee carries the pollen to the flowers of another plant.

Now those flowers can produce seeds.

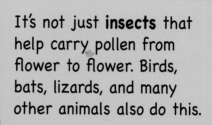

It's not just **insects** that help carry pollen from flower to flower. Birds, bats, lizards, and many other animals also do this.

Honeybee

Pollen

Let's Talk

Why do you think bees, butterflies, and other insects visit flowers?

A Flower's Sweet Treat

How do flowers attract their animal helpers?

Flowers produce a sweet liquid called **nectar**.

Bees, butterflies, and other animals visit flowers to feed on nectar.

Let's Talk

Honeybees carry some nectar and pollen back to their hives. Why do you think they do this?

(The answer is at the bottom of the page.)

Answer: Inside their hives, honeybees turn nectar into honey. They eat honey in winter, when there are no flowers around. Bees feed pollen to their young.

A butterfly feeding on nectar

A flower's smell and colorful petals tell insects that there is nectar inside.

Be a Scientist!

On a warm, dry spring or summer day, go bee watching in a yard, garden, or park.

1. Count the number of bees on each type of plant.

What color flowers are the most popular?

Do the popular flowers have a strong smell?

2. Use a watch or phone to time a bee for one minute.

How many flowers does the bee visit in that time?

3. Use a magnifying glass to look closely at the flowers.

Do you observe any sticky nectar or dusty pollen inside?

BE CAREFUL!
Go bee watching with an adult. Do not disturb the bees. Do not touch the bees or put your face close to them.

All About Seeds

Seeds form inside protective coverings.

Apple tree seeds and tomato plant seeds are surrounded by soft fruits.

Seed

Apple

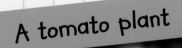

A tomato plant

Seeds form inside a flower.

A soft fruit forms around the seeds.

The fruit becomes a fat, red tomato.

Tomato plant seeds

Sunflower seed

Shell

Sunflower seeds have a hard shell.

Poppy seeds form inside a hard pod.

Poppy

Seedpod

Seeds

Spiky casing

The seeds of a horse chestnut tree grow inside spiky casings.

Seed

Cones and Seeds

Some plants, such as pine trees, don't grow flowers. Instead, they produce cones.

Some of a pine tree's cones release pollen into the air.

Pollen cone

Pollen

Scots pine tree

Other cones produce seeds.

Seed cone

Once pollen lands on the seed cones, seeds begin to form.

When the seeds are fully formed, the cone's woody scales open to release the seeds into the air.

Scales

The seed cone turns brown.

Seed

Be a Scientist!

Pine tree seeds must be released in dry weather so they can float in the air. If it is rainy or the air is damp, the seeds won't float. Let's investigate cones and seeds!

Gather your equipment:
- A cone with open scales
- A jar with a lid
- Water
- A notebook and pen

How does a cone stop its seeds from being released in wet weather? Write your ideas in a notebook

1. Put the cone in the jar.

2. Fill the jar with water so the cone is covered. Screw the lid on tight and leave for several hours.

What do you observe happens? Record the results in your notebook. Did the results match your ideas?

3. Next, remove the cone from the jar and place it somewhere warm.

What do you think will happen now?

What Do Seedlings Need?

Seedlings need a place to grow where there is soil, water, **nutrients**, and sunshine.

Seedlings may struggle to grow if they are too close to their parent plant and other seedlings.

Seedling

The parent plant may block out sunlight.

Soil

There may not be enough water and nutrients in the soil for all the plants.

It's important that seedlings have space to grow away from their parent plant and each other.

Too crowded!

If too many seedlings try to grow in the same spot, many of the little plants will die.

Space to grow!

Let's Talk

How do you think a plant spreads its seeds to new growing places?

Seeds on the Move

Many plants get help from animals to spread their seeds to new growing places. How?

Bramble plant

A fox eating blackberries

Animals eat berries and other fruit that contain seeds.

An animal's body digests the soft fruit, but the hard seeds pass through.

The seeds leave an animal's body in its poop—often far from the parent plant!

Fox poop containing bramble seeds

Seeds

Some seeds have hooks and hairs that attach to animals and people. Then the seeds hitch a ride to a new growing place.

Hooks

Goosegrass attached to a sweater

Blown by the Wind

Some seeds float on the wind to a new growing place.

A dandelion flower produces up to 400 seeds.

Each seed has a fluffy parachute that helps it float away from its parent plant.

Dandelion flower

Parachute

Seed

The longer a seed floats in the air, the farther it can travel from its parent plant.

The seeds of a sycamore tree have wings like helicopter blades.

The wings help the seeds whirl and spin through the air.

Sycamore seed

Wing

Let's Test It!

What shape of seed do you think will float best in the wind?

Gather your equipment and materials:
- A notebook and pen
- Scissors
- Glue
- Craft materials such as beads, feathers, paper, string, modeling clay
- Tape measure

1. Write down your ideas and draw your seed design.

2. Use the materials to make your design.

3. Choose a spot to stand. Place your seed on the palm of your hand. Blow hard on the seed.

How far did the seed travel? Measure the distance and record your result.

What changes would you make to your seed design to help it travel farther?

4. Make your new design and test it!

Eating Seeds and Fruit

Many of the foods we eat are seeds and fruit.

Mini corn on the cob

Seeds

A fruit is any plant part that contains seeds. We might think of cucumbers, peppers, and tomatoes as vegetables, but they are actually fruits.

Cucumber seeds

Seedpod

Peas are the seeds of a pea plant.

Strawberry seeds

Walnut tree seed

Pumpkin seeds

Lentils are seeds.

Cherry

Cherry tree seed

Kiwi fruit seeds

Avocado

Seed

Pepper seeds

A bagel with black poppy seeds

Orange seed

Peanut plant seeds

The peanut plant grows from here.

Have you ever noticed a tiny squiggly part inside a peanut?

This is the part that grows into a new peanut plant.

27

More Seeds to Eat!

Which of these foods do you think are made from seeds?

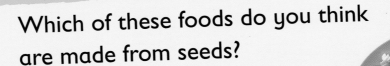

Bread

Oatmeal

Pasta

Rice

They all are!

Oatmeal is made from the seeds of oat plants.

Wheat

When you eat rice, you're eating rice plant seeds.

The seeds of wheat plants are made into flour for baking bread, cookies, and cakes.

Wheat seeds are also used to make pasta dough.

Cutters are used to make the dough into shapes.

Pasta dough

Cutters

Wheat, rice, and oats are types of grass plants. The seeds of these plants are known as **grains**.

Check It Out!

What seeds and fruits have you eaten this week?

Make a list in a notebook.

Remember to include foods made from grains.

Toast and strawberry jam

From a Tiny Seed

Most seeds fall from their parent plant in summer. They settle in the soil and wait for spring to begin growing.

A dandelion plant grows fast.

It produces leaves, flowers, and seeds in just a few weeks.

Dandelion seedling

Dandelion plant

Most trees grow slowly. Some types of trees live for hundreds or even thousands of years!

This is a giant sequoia tree. It is more than 2,000 years old and is the largest tree on Earth. It grew from a seed that was smaller than a baked bean!

Glossary

grains (GRAYNZ)
The seeds of grass plants, such as wheat and rice, that people eat.

insect (IN-sekt)
An animal with six legs, a body in three sections, and a hard shell called an exoskeleton.

nectar (NEK-tur)
A sweet liquid made by flowers.

nutrient (NOO-tree-uhnt)
A substance that a living thing needs to grow and be healthy. Plants usually take in nutrients from soil through their roots.

pollen (POL-uhn)
A colored dust that is made by flowers and cones, and is needed for making seeds.

roots (ROOTS)
Underground parts of a plant that take in water and nutrients from the soil.

seedling (SEED-ling)
A new, young plant that sprouts from a seed.

shoot (SHOOT)
A new part of a plant. Shoots grow from seeds and from existing plants.

Index

MAY   2017